FORTITER ET FIDELITER

Ormesby Hall

Middlesbrough

THE NATIONAL TRUST

Town and country

Ormesby Hall is an extraordinary survival. When John Graves visited in 1808, the house and its surrounding parkland were at the centre of a large farming estate stretching up to the banks of the River Tees. Today, they stand alone, as a rural enclave in the suburbs of Middlesbrough.

For nearly 400 years, Ormesby was the home of the Pennyman family, who acquired the estate in the early 17th century. The present house was built for James and Dorothy Pennyman in the 1740s, but it incorporates parts of the earlier house within its service wing. From the outside, it is restrained and austere. However, its glory lies inside, with fine plasterwork and carved woodwork interiors from two periods of the 18th century: the bold Palladian decoration of the 1740s contrasts with more delicate Neo-classical plasterwork ceilings in the Drawing and Dining Rooms, commissioned by Sir James Pennyman, 6th Bt, in the 1770s. The 6th Baronet also built the imposing stable block and laid out the park, with its plantations and main entrance lodge.

Ruin and retrenchment

The 6th Baronet had a rich inheritance, with estates in Stainton, Tunstall, Maltby and Sadberge, and houses at Thornton and Beverley, as well as at Ormesby. However, he spent large sums on politics and gambling and went bankrupt in 1792. All the contents of Ormesby Hall were auctioned to pay off his creditors, and the house was shut up for sixteen years. The family fortunes never fully recovered from his recklessness, and his successors had limited resources to invest in their home. His son, Sir William Pennyman, 7th Bt, reclaimed the Hall and built the East Lodge in the 1820s, but made few other improvements to the property. He left most of

The Ormesby parkland is a rural oasis in the southern outskirts of Middlesbrough, which lies beyond the trees

A political rally at Ormesby in 1937, which was attended by the Prime Minister, Neville Chamberlain

his personal possessions to his sister's family, but his heir, James White (Worsley) Pennyman, bought back several items of furniture for Ormesby. James White started to lease land at the northern end of the estate for housing associated with the new town of Middlesbrough, to make the estate a more viable proposition. He and his son, James Stovin, made the final alterations to Ormesby Hall, adding the front porch, the Dining Room extension and the block connecting the service wing and main building.

Concerned landowners

Though the estate shrank from the mid-19th century, the Victorian Pennymans were dedicated landowners, living on the Ormesby estate all year round and immersing themselves in the life of the local community. This pattern continued into the 20th century, even though most of the people on Teesside now depended on industry rather than the land. Colonel James Pennyman set up imaginative schemes to help unemployed miners during the Great Depression of the 1930s. His wife, Ruth, promoted the arts in the area and set up local drama groups, so that Ormesby became known for its theatrical productions. Their projects attracted the composer Michael Tippett and the innovative theatre director Joan Littlewood to Ormesby.

Colonel Pennyman had been forced to sell land in the 1920s to pay death-duties, and the remainder of the Ormesby estate was compulsorily purchased after the Second World War. When the Colonel died without children in 1961, he left Ormesby Hall, its parkland and home farm to the National Trust. His widow, Ruth, lived on at Ormesby and continued to pursue her theatrical activities until her death in 1983.

Tour of the House

The Exterior

The main, three-storey house was built for James and Dorothy Pennyman between about 1740 and 1745. This plain block of five bays by four, constructed of warm Jurassic sandstone, was designed in a simple version of the Palladian style, though the hipped roof and overhanging eaves hark back to such late 17th-century houses as Belton in Lincolnshire. On the main north and south façades, the central three-bay section projects under a pediment, to emphasise the triple rhythm that was such an important element of Palladian design. In addition, the pediment on the north side encloses the Pennyman coat of arms. The sandstone is enlivened with a fine parallel-tooled finish, which is characteristic of the north-east of England.

The front porch was added by James White Pennyman in 1855. The block connecting the Old Wing and main house was also started by James White about 1855, but it was greatly extended by James Stovin Pennyman in 1879. He added the second storey and the rather cumbersome porch on the east side, with a rusticated and arcaded ground floor. The bay window to the rear of the house was built as an extension to the Dining Room by the Atkinson partnership of York for James Stovin in 1871.

The Interior

After the 6th Baronet, none of the later Pennymans was a dedicated collector, and the present contents of the house represent an *ad hoc* accumulation of family items since the early 19th century. There is much solid and

comfortable country-house furniture, with a few outstanding 18th-century items, possibly acquired through marriage in the late 19th century. From the mid-19th century, the Pennymans treated Ormesby Hall as a comfortable family home and as a base for their numerous local activities and projects. Colonel and Mrs Pennyman frequently opened their home to local arts groups and travelling musicians and actors, and as long as the house was structurally sound, they were not too concerned with decoration and display. Since Ruth died in 1983, the National Trust has made very few changes to the interior of the house, and the decorations and furnishings are maintained in the spirit of the family.

(Right)
A watercolour of the Entrance Hall in the late 19th century, when the columns were painted red (North-East Bedroom)

(Opposite page)
The entrance front and stables

(Below)
The entrance front. The Old Wing is to the left

The Entrance Hall

This room, created for Dorothy Pennyman in the 1740s, is at the heart of the house, giving access to the Library, Drawing Room and Dining Room on the south and west, and the Den, Study and Staircase Hall on the east. In the late 18th century it was very simply furnished, with a bare stone floor and hall-chairs arranged around the edge of the room for waiting servants. By the late 19th century, it had become an informal living room, filled with oak furniture, rugs and paintings, as well as a number of hunting trophies (which have since been removed to the Staircase Hall).

It was a room to gather in, for parties of gentlemen before shoots, and house guests before dinner, with a fire blazing in the grate during the winter months. In later years, it was used as a venue for concerts and lectures organised by the Ormesby and Eston Guild of Arts, under Ruth Pennyman's chairmanship.

Design and decoration

The perfectly symmetrical columned Entrance Hall is a model of Palladian planning. The symmetry is emphasised by the ceiling plaster-work in which a circle surrounds a central square.

The bold decorative plaster and woodwork include typically Palladian motifs, such as the carved oak wreaths on the doorcases and frieze, and Vitruvian scrolls (wave pattern) on the dado. Their robust quality and profusion are remarkable in a provincial gentry house.

The Entrance Hall was redecorated by the National Trust in the mid-1970s, on the advice of the interior decorator John Fowler.

Locks

Dorothy Pennyman was clearly very proud of her locks, as she mentions them specifically in her Will of 1754. Her brass 'rim' locks, mounted on the face of the doors, survive here. In rooms redecorated in the 1770s, the doors have 'mortice' locks hidden within the thickness of the wood, with small 'snib' (or latch) handles on the inside face, to provide privacy.

Furnishings

The present furnishings represent a thinning-out from the Edwardian period. Much of the oak furniture is 19th-century in the 17th-century style, though *the settle* to the right of the fireplace incorporates the headboard of a 17th-century bed. *The settle* to the left of the fireplace is a genuine 17th-century piece, as is the chest, which was made in west Yorkshire.

Pictures

The seascape, from the studio of the celebrated 17th-century marine artist William van der Velde, is probably the work of one of his pupils, J. van Hagen. The naïve painting of a hunt to the right of the fireplace is probably English, c.1740, and the rustic scene opposite is a copy after the 17th-century Dutch artist Aelbert Cuyp. The portraits on either side of the Dining Room door are of James Worsley Pennyman (1856–1924) and his wife, Dora Maria.

Heraldry

The two carved stone lions, on either side of the front door, represent the Pennyman crest, with a hole through the middle for a wooden spear, which has long since disintegrated. They were made for the gate-piers at the entrance to the park c.1772 and, unusually, retain some of their original paintwork. To protect this, they were installed in the Entrance Hall in 1994.

Over the carved mantelpiece is the *Pennyman coat of arms*, bearing the family crest and the 'red hand of Ulster', denoting the baronetcy created in 1664. The baronetcy expired in 1852, when the Ormesby estate passed to the Worsley family through the female line.

Ceramics and weapons

The pair of oriental vases on the mantel is decorated with a technique known as 'clobbering' (overpainting an already glazed and fired piece with lacquer and other colours that do not need re-firing). *The carriage pistols* on the chest are Britannia silver-mounted and are dated 1723.

The Entrance Hall

The Library

This was the 'Breakfasting Room' in the late 18th century and then the 'Ante-Room' to the Dining Room until 1871. It became known as the Library in the late 19th century, but it was generally used as a gentleman's smoking room, where the men gathered late in the evening, after the wives and female guests had gone to bed. At about 10.30pm, the men went upstairs to put on smoking coats and came down here to smoke their pipes, drink whisky and soda and play the odd round of whist. Smoking was forbidden anywhere else in the house, except in the Dining Room after dinner. The padded door was installed in the Victorian period to prevent the sounds of conversation disturbing the household at night. After Colonel Pennyman died in 1961, Mrs Pennyman used the Library as a winter sitting room, moving the Victorian walnut desk here from the Drawing Room each winter and back again in the summer. Though it was cosier here than in the Drawing Room, the house was always very cold in winter, as Mrs Pennyman never used any supplementary heating.

Decoration

The panelling, cornice and carved overmantel date from the 1740s and are of the same high quality as the work in the Entrance Hall. The scallop shells in the cornice and swags of flowers in the overmantel are particularly fine.

Books

The 6th Baronet's books were sold at auction in 1792. The later Pennymans were not voracious readers, but the books in the Library indicate some of their interests in the late 19th and 20th centuries. In particular, the collection of books on Marxism and Soviet Russia reflects Ruth Pennyman's interest in left-wing politics.

Furniture

The furniture is largely Victorian, except for the Pembroke table behind the sofa and the large mahogany break-front bookcase, which are late 18th-century.

Pictures

The portrait over the fireplace is of Colonel A. E. Pennyman, Colonel Pennyman's much-loved Uncle Alfie. *The 1969 abstract*, to the right of the fireplace, is by Tom MacGuiness, an artist much admired by Mrs Pennyman. *The portrait* of Colonel Pennyman to the left of the large break-front bookcase is by Alec Wright and dated 1953. *The miniature* on the desk is of Mrs Greville Knight, Mrs Pennyman's mother. *The engravings* are a series of Venetian views by Visentini after Canaletto.

   The framed illuminated manuscript on the table by the door is the grant of the family crest to James Pennyman of 1599.

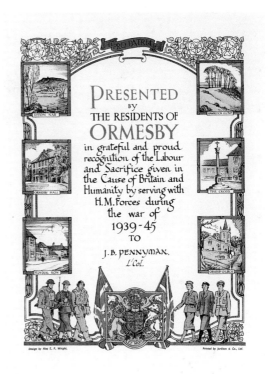

Jim Pennyman's service in the National Defence Corps during the Second World War was remembered in this presentation, which illustrates places of local interest (on show in the Library)

The Pennymans' library includes works on Soviet Russia by Leon Trotsky and Sidney and Beatrice Webb

The Drawing Room

This room, originally Dorothy Pennyman's 'Best Eating Parlour', was remodelled by Sir James Pennyman, 6th Bt, *c.*1772, to form a fashionable dining room. It was converted into a drawing room in 1871 under the influence of James Stovin Pennyman's mother-in-law, Mrs Coltman, who lived at Ormesby in her later years and made many improvements towards the comfort of the house.

The ladies gathered here immediately after dinner, to be joined by the gentlemen 45 minutes later, when there was usually singing, piano-playing and games. In Stovin's time, the games were rather serious and educational, based on guessing the origin of a quotation or the name of a famous artist or writer.

Decoration and design

The plasterwork ceiling dates from the 1770s and may well have been executed by John Henderson, to the designs of John Carr of York (see p. 37). The delicacy of the work and the complexity of its design make an interesting contrast with the earlier, bolder decoration in the Entrance Hall and Library. The tiny masks of Bacchus, Roman god of wine, which emerge from beribboned medallions, reflect the convivial atmosphere of Sir James's dining room.

There were originally two further supporting columns, between the half-Corinthian columns at the north end of the room, forming a screen in front of the dining-room sideboard. They were removed, probably in 1871, but one, in reduced form, now serves as a lamp-stand.

Fireplace

The fireplace surround, with its carved fret pattern, dates from the 1740s, while the over-mantel, with its urns and swagged husks, was installed in the 1770s.

Furniture

Notable pieces of furniture include the French Rococo kingwood parquetry *commode* with gilt bronze mounts and a marble top, opposite the door from the Entrance Hall. This piece is signed by Roussel, who was a Parisian cabinet-maker of the mid-18th century. A Regency chiffonier (chest-of-drawers) with brass columns supporting the bookshelves stands between the windows, and an early 19th-century writing-chest with a fall-front, which has lost its upper section of bookshelves, is in the corner of the room. The suite of oval-backed painted armchairs and window seats is in the French taste, although it was made in England *c.*1780. The little painted side-chairs, upholstered *en suite,* are late 19th-century and were made by Maple & Co.

Pictures

The group portrait after Romney, over the fireplace, is late 18th-century, although the children are depicted in 17th-century 'Van Dyck' dress, and the composition owes much

The French parquetry commode in the Drawing Room

The Drawing Room

to that artist's portrait of the children of King
Charles I. The sitters are the children of the
White family, one of whom, Lydia, married a
Worsley. Her son, James White Pennyman,
succeeded to Ormesby after the death of the
7th Baronet in 1852.

The oval portrait to the left of the fireplace is
attributed to Philippe Mercier and is probably
of Bridget Gee, the mother of the 6th Baronet.
Mercier was a celebrated French portrait
painter who was taken up by Frederick, Prince
of Wales and much patronised by fashionable
society. This portrait was almost certainly
painted between 1739 and 1751, when Mercier
was living in York.

The pair of portraits on the north wall is of
Colonel and Mrs Pennyman and was painted
by Mills in 1958.

*The late 18th-century portraits of William
Joseph Coltman and his wife, Mary*, on the
window walls, came to Ormesby as a result of
the marriage of James Stovin Pennyman to
Mary Coltman in 1855. The portrait to the
right, on the short window wall, is of Michael
Warton of Beverley, an ancestor of Mary
Warton; she married Sir James Pennyman,
3rd Bt, in 1692 and was the mother of the
builder of the present house.

Ceramics

The collection of *blue-and-white Chinese export
porcelain* gathered around the tureen at the
near end of the room is all that remains of a
fine late 18th-century dinner service. The pair
of *19th-century German candlesticks* is modelled
as male and female figures in the 18th-century
Rococo style.

The Dining Room

The Dining Room

This room was totally refurbished by Sir James Pennyman c.1772, to form a splendid saloon on the central axis of the house. He furnished it elegantly with chairs and sofas covered in green silk, but after the 1792 auction it was left empty, and used by James White Pennyman and his children for games and dancing in the evening. In 1871 it was converted into a dining parlour by James Stovin Pennyman (on the advice of Mrs Coltman), who commis-sioned the Atkinson partnership of York to extend the room, with a bay window over-looking the garden. The new arrangement of rooms allowed much better access from the Kitchen to the Dining Room, with a service passage leading directly from the Old Wing to the door to the right of the fireplace.

Colonel Pennyman recalled that in his grandfather's time dinner was served precisely at 8 o'clock and late comers were barely tolerated. At 7.55pm and 7.58pm, an electric bell sounded on the 1st- and 2nd-floor landings to warn visitors to come downstairs, and the gong was struck on the first stroke of the hour, when the Butler announced dinner and the party entered the Dining Room. After dinner, the gentlemen lingered at the table, drinking port and smoking cigars, while the ladies retired to the Drawing Room. The Dining Room was still used for dancing on big family occasions, when the furniture was cleared away and French chalk rubbed into the floorboards. On Colonel Pennyman's coming-of-age in 1904, it accommodated over 70 guests, dancing until 3 in the morning to the strains of Johnson Laird's band from Middlesbrough.

Decoration

The plasterwork ceiling of Sir James's saloon encompasses the whole of the original room in one design, with the concentrated interlacing of the central circle giving the impression of a crowning dome. The 19th-century cornice in the bay window is a less accomplished imitation of the 18th-century work, but the stencilled scallops of the frieze, reminiscent of valencing on a railway platform canopy, are a delightful decorative addition. The lower central pane in the bay window can be raised to give access to the garden.

Furniture

The present furniture is largely mahogany of the late 18th and early 19th centuries. *The cellarette* under the sideboard is, as its name suggests, a mini-cellar, formerly lined with lead, for keeping wine at an even cool temperature. One of the pedestal cupboards in the bay is fitted as a hot cupboard, with a zinc lining, and the other has provision for a chamberpot.

Pictures

Over the fireplace hangs *the portrait of the 6th Baronet*, painted in 1762, eight years before he inherited Ormesby and the title. The painting is attributed to Joshua Reynolds, with whom Sir James is known to have had three sittings in October of that year. To the left of the fireplace is a copy of Reynolds's painting of

the daughters of the architect James Paine. Their mother was an ancestor of Dora Maria Beaumont, who married James Worsley Pennyman in 1882. The original, which was painted as a pendant to Reynolds's famous portrait of James Paine and his son, was sold by Dora Maria's father in 1906, when the present copy was made. Subsequently, the figure of Mrs Paine was painted out in both the original and the copy. The Lady Lever Art Gallery, which owns the original painting, had the figure revealed *c.*1935.

On the opposite wall, *members of the Beaumont family* are shown in a copy of a group portrait by George Romney. *The two 19th-century portraits* on either side of the door by H. P. Briggs depict Mr and Mrs Thomas Lee of Barnstaple in Devon, ancestors of Ruth Pennyman.

Silver (on sideboard)

The silver race cup was commissioned by Sir James Pennyman, the racing 6th Baronet, and his co-steward at Northallerton race-course, Thomas Pearce, at a cost of £50. It was presented in 1772 to a horse called Nutcracker, owned by William Fenwick of Bywell Castle, Northumberland, and descended through a branch of his family until 1981, when it was purchased for Ormesby Hall by the National Trust.

Other silver includes a salver presented to Dora Maria Beaumont on her marriage to James Worsley Pennyman in 1882. The silver dessert service was presented to their son at his majority in 1904.

Ceramics and metalwork

The ceramics on the mantelpiece are early Wedgwood Krater basalt ware, *c.*1790. The remains of a dinner service on the table near the window is of the Davenport 'cabbage leaf' design. The 19th-century dessert service on the dining-table is decorated in the Japanese Imari pattern and is possibly also Davenport. The figures of horses on the side-tables are of a cast zinc form known as spelter, which was popular in the 19th century as a cheap alternative to cast bronze.

The Den

The Den

Since the late 19th century, this has been used as the estate room, known variously as the Gun Room, the Map Room and the Den. The 19th-century maps, showing the extent of the estate, have hung here on rollers for at least a century; the pine stand, supporting croquet mallets and balls and odd bits of cricketing paraphernalia, for almost as long. In later years, Colonel Pennyman kept hand tools for gardening and forestry work here, when the adjacent room was his study.

The Study

Historically, this room has been a governess's room and small or informal dining room, although towards the end of the 19th century it was the schoolroom. For a short period, in the 1870s, it was used for Sunday services, while St Cuthbert's church was being refurbished. Finally, in the 1920s, it became Colonel Pennyman's study, where he spent at least an hour every morning after breakfast, writing letters and organising estate affairs. As far as possible, the room is shown as he used it, although his desk has not survived.

Decoration

The boldly moulded cornice and doorcases and finely carved overmantel suggest that this was originally a significant room, on a par with the Library in the opposite corner. The Delftware (tin-glazed earthenware) tiles on the fireplace cheeks were made in England in the late 18th century, possibly in the Liverpool factory.

Furniture

The oak cupboard, to the left of the fireplace, was made by the estate joiner in the 1930s and contained the Colonel's filing system. The labels on the pigeon holes inside the cupboard, ranging from 'North Ormesby Hospital' and 'Teesside Industrial' to 'Church Assembly' and 'Village Hall', demonstrate the breadth of his local interests. The chair at the desk is from the short-lived factory at Boosbeck funded by Colonel Pennyman in the early 1930s (see p. 43), and has the stark lines typical of the factory's output. The oak armorial chairs, decorated with the Pennymans' crest, are part of a larger set, dating from the 19th century.

Photographs

They include one of the Colonel's father, James Worsley Pennyman, over the mantel-piece. He compiled *The Pennyman Records*

(1904), a series of essays and archival extracts on the history of the Pennyman family.

The framed document (on the wall opposite the window) lists the tenants of Ormesby Hall who subscribed to Colonel Pennyman's coming-of-age present in 1904. The border features photographs of the Colonel, his parents and Ormesby Hall.

The montage of eight photographs shows places in and about Trinity College, Cambridge, which was attended by both Colonel Pennyman and his father.

The Staircase Hall

The fine oak staircase has three turned balusters to each tread and the balustrade terminates at the bottom in an elegant volute. Adjacent to it is the service staircase (down which you later descend). It was fairly common practice in the 18th century for the main and service staircases to rise side-by-side in the centre of one of the side elevations.

Furniture

The 18th-century oak longcase clock was retailed by Stapylton of Middleham, Yorkshire, though the case is probably a later replacement.

Pictures

The pair of 18th-century portraits at the top of the stairs is of Mr and Mrs Francis Hugonin, ancestors of Francis Hugonin, who married Joan Pennyman, the Colonel's first cousin, in 1925. Francis Hugonin senior left Switzerland to work in India in 1700 and emigrated to England in about 1720. The East Indiaman in the background of his portrait may be a reference to his trading activities.

Heating

The first cast-iron radiator on the landing is all that remains of the original heating system. The other radiator, in a similar style, was installed by the National Trust to provide conservation heating.

(Left) The chair in the Study is a Boosbeck design

The North-East Bedroom

The door immediately adjacent to the top of the stairs leads to the first of three guest bedrooms on the north side of the Gallery. From the mid-19th century, the Worsley Pennymans regularly held house parties of extended family and friends, who came to stay for hunting, shooting and the Redcar races. In addition to these rooms on the first floor, they refurbished several guest bedrooms on the attic storey and, on big occasions, such as Frances Pennyman's wedding to Colonel Macbean in 1855, accommodated bachelor guests in the Old Wing. The dressing bell sounded at 7.30pm, to warn visitors to change for dinner. Colonel Pennyman recalled that, in his grandfather's time, the gentlemen put on white tie and tails and the ladies décolleté dresses and their finest jewellery, if there was any kind of party.

Decoration

This room was decorated c.1740 in a much plainer style than the other guest bedrooms. The fireplace has a Vitruvian scroll frieze and overmantel carved in the manner of the Palladian architect William Kent.

Furniture

The early 19th-century mahogany four-poster bed is hung with blue chintz to match the chair covers and window curtains. The late 18th-century chest-of-drawers conceals a night commode; the top two drawers are false and lift away to reveal the fitted interior.

Watercolours

The amateur watercolours are probably late 19th-century and show views of Ormesby Hall, including the Entrance Hall, hung with hunting trophies, and the garden with conservatories.

A fragment of 18th-century flock wallpaper was found preserved in the Dressing Room

The Dressing Room

This little room served as a dressing room to the North-East Bedroom in the late 18th century and as a linen room in the mid-19th century, when the wall-cupboards were installed. The present curtains suggest that it was the dressing room to the North Bedroom in later years.

Furniture

The small single bed in the style of c.1840 has recently been rehung with modern dimity fabric. The Regency giltwood mirror is similar to others in the house.

Engravings

The set of early 19th-century engravings on the wall opposite the window shows places connected with the battle of Waterloo.

Ceramics

The figures of Dick Turpin and Tom King on the mantelpiece are 19th-century Staffordshire earthenware.

The North Bedroom

The North Bedroom

This is the best guest bedroom and stands in the centre of the north front over the Entrance Hall. As befits its status, the architectural decoration is in the best manner of Dorothy Pennyman's craftsmen. The overmantel is supported on console brackets, with carved husks hanging in drops below.

Furniture

The four-poster bed is one of a pair of Regency mahogany beds in the house, both carved with elegant acanthus leaf capitals. The dark, heavily patterned hangings are probably Edwardian.

The large mahogany clothes press on the opposite wall, which has been altered internally to create a wardrobe, is also early 19th-century. The rest of the furniture is largely Victorian, including the fine burr-walnut veneered writing-table with its barley-sugar supports. The curious painted corner cupboard originated at Walsingham Abbey in Norfolk.

Pictures

The pastel drawings by G. L. Browning depict members of the Pennyman and Coltman families. The drawing over the mantelpiece is of James Stovin Pennyman, dating from 1851.

The North-West Dressing Room

This room, formerly two, was made into one in the late 19th century. The inner part, which lacks decoration, was originally a 'dark' dressing- or powder-closet, with access to the landing through one of the gib doors. In the 1850s, the outer part was used by Stovin's sister Frances as a private sitting room, where Colonel Macbean proposed to her.

Watercolours

A group of four watercolours by various hands shows Beeston Castle in Cheshire and the island of Corfu where James White Worsley (later Pennyman) worked as a civil engineer before he inherited Ormesby.

The North-West Bedroom

This was originally created as a bedroom or dressing room, but it was used as the family sitting room in the 1850s and '60s, while the saloon (present Dining Room) on the ground floor was left empty for dancing and games. It was redecorated as a guest bedroom in the late 19th century, when the present Drawing Room was formed.

Chimneypiece

The fluted marble fireplace surround and frieze of anthemions above were installed in the 1770s, while the overmantel dates from the earlier period of decoration, in the 1740s. The still-life painting in the over-mantel is typical of a style of decorative painting popular in the late 17th and early 18th centuries.

Furniture

The pelmet boards are oddly Egyptian in feel and must date from the early 19th century. The bed, of similar date, matches the one in the North Bedroom. Also from the Regency period is the settee at the end of the bed and,

slightly earlier, *the curious 'estate' desk* in the window bay, with its multiplicity of lidded compartments and hinged wells. The caned chairs with punched brass decoration date from *c.*1830. The mid-18th-century mahogany chest-of-drawers on the west wall is the top of a larger 'chest on chest' with turned legs added later. One of the pair of French Rococo *armoires* (wardrobes) contains a note of their delivery by train to the 'Pennyman sidings' in 1904.

The Ante-Room

Situated between the guest and family rooms, this room was used as an informal sitting room or music room in the late 18th century, equipped with a Kirckman harpsichord, bass

Bridget Pennyman, the mother of 'the wicked Sir James' Pennyman, 6th Bt (Ante-Room)

violin, backgammon board and work-table. It was renamed the Ante-Room in the mid-19th century, when the North-West Bedroom became the family sitting room. For Colonel Pennyman's coming-of-age party in 1904, 76 guests dined in the Ante-Room and Gallery, with the Dining Room being used for dancing later in the evening.

Doorcase and chimneypiece

The formal pedimented doorcase emphasises the communal nature of this room, in contrast to the private bedrooms and dressing rooms on either side. The restrained Neo-classical fire-surround, dating from the 1770s, encloses a slightly later hob grate, c.1830.

Furniture

The set of oval cane-seated armchairs, c.1800, is very finely carved, retaining its original painted and gilt finish. *The burr walnut centre-table* and *mahogany side-table*, both with marquetry decoration, date from the 19th century. The latter imitates the style of the late 17th century in the Netherlands, which influenced English taste. The early 19th-century *mahogany break-front bookcase* is of fine quality. It contains the 1854–96 diaries of James Stovin Pennyman, which record much of the daily life of Ormesby in the Victorian period.

The so-called 'Armada' chest, under the window, is a 17th-century safe box, in which Sir James Pennyman, 6th Bt, is supposed to have inherited £30,000 in 1770 (though he had clearly squandered his fortune by 1792). As is common with such chests, the real keyhole is concealed in the strapwork of the lid, the keyhole visible on the front being false.

Pictures

The group of seven small mid-18th-century oval portraits, depicting the family of Sir James Pennyman, 6th Bt, is attributed to a follower of the English society portrait painter John Downman. Sir James's mother, Bridget (née

Looking across to Bamburgh from Lindisfarne Castle; by Len Tabner (Reading Room)

Gee), and his father, Ralph, are to the left of the Gallery door, and his brother-in-law, Hugh Bethell, and four of his children on the right. The landscape painting is by the 17th-century Dutch artist Adam Pynacker.

The Reading Room

This room, originally designed as a bedroom, was used by Ruth Pennyman as a study, where she wrote poetry at a desk in the window. In the mid-1990s, it was redecorated by the National Trust as a reading room, where you are welcome to sit and read or study the exhibition of contemporary art.

Foundation for Art

In the spirit of Ruth Pennyman, who was an enthusiastic patron of young artists, the Reading Room is hung with modern paintings from the permanent collection of the National Trust's Foundation for Art. The Foundation commissions work from contemporary artists, reflecting the work of the Trust and inspired by its properties. Some of the paintings are by Len Tabner, a well-known local artist, who documents the landscape and industry of Teesside.

The Gallery

The Gallery, or main landing at the head of the stairs, runs east–west across the centre of the house and serves all the principal bed-rooms. It is one of the unexpected delights of Ormesby, containing some of the finest carved work from both periods of 18th-century decoration in the house. The columns at the head of the stairs, with acanthus leaf capitals, were installed *c*.1772, probably under the direction of John Carr of York. Their design seems to derive from the Temple of the Four Winds in Athens, engravings of which had been published a few years earlier by James 'Athenian' Stuart.

The series of sumptuously carved doorcases was executed in the earlier period, by Dorothy Pennyman's fine provincial craftsmen. Each pair is distinguished by subtle differences in form and pattern, which reflect the status of the rooms beyond. The large curved segmental pediments and Corinthian columns herald the grandest guest bedroom on the north side and the principal family bedroom on the south. The more restrained Ionic pilasters and broken pediment at the far end of the Gallery mark the Ante-Room as the only other 'public' space on the first floor. The simplest doorcases, to the right and left at the top of the stairs, lack pilasters altogether, as they lead to the smallest guest bedroom and the back staircase.

Jib doors

Beyond the central north and south doors is a pair of secret 'jib' doors giving direct access

The Gallery

to the small closets and dressing rooms that separate the main bedrooms from each other.

Furniture

The Regency cane-seated dining-chairs are painted to simulate rosewood. The painted side-tables, from the same period, support a collection of Victorian stationery and jewellery boxes.

Pictures

Of *the four portraits* at the far end of the Gallery, the one to the left on the left-hand wall is of Sir Thomas Pennyman, 2nd Bt, while the others represent members of the Beaumont family, ancestors of Dora Maria Beaumont, who married James Worsley Pennyman in 1882.

The pair of portraits at the near end of the Gallery is of the Rev. William Pennyman, Colonel Pennyman's uncle, and his wife Beatrix.

Lighting

The 'Menorah' lights were acquired by Ruth Pennyman in the East End of London during the Second World War, when ordinary light-fittings were hard to obtain.

The South Bedroom

This appears to have been used as the principal family bedroom since the 1740s. It is recorded in 1853 as having been Sir William Pennyman's room and was used by Ruth Pennyman as her bedroom in the 20th century. In common with the other family rooms on the south front, the decoration is much plainer than in the guest rooms on the north side.

Furniture

The early 19th-century mahogany bed is painted with a later terracotta colour to match a bedroom suite of red lacquer, bequeathed away from Ormesby on Mrs Pennyman's death in

The South Bedroom

1983. *The grand Rococo pier-glass* matches one in the North Bedroom. *The laundry basket* in the corner was made at the Boosbeck furniture factory, set up by Colonel Pennyman to give work to local unemployed men in the 1930s (see p. 43).

Pictures

The Indian miniature, c.1600, to the left of the bed, depicts *The Peaceable Kingdom* and *The Solomonic Throne*. It may have been acquired by Colonel Pennyman on a trip to India c.1904.

Descend one flight of the back stairs to the first floor of the linking passage between the main house and the Old Wing, built by James Stovin Pennyman in 1871.

Passing housekeeper's cupboards and closets, ascend another flight of stairs to the first floor of the Old Wing, where there is a display of model railways and other changing exhibitions. The model railways, which were developed by a group of volunteers at Ormesby Hall in the 1990s, may be of particular interest to younger visitors. The Corfe Castle layout, representing a branch line of the London & South-eastern Railway in the 1920s, was donated by Mr Ron Rising in 1995.

Then descend to the ground floor of the Old Wing, which contains the Great Kitchen, Laundry, tea-room (the former Servants' Hall) and shop.

The Old Wing

The Old Wing is a two-storey quadrangle to the east of the main house, and contains parts of the Pennymans' original house, built about 1601. The earliest part of the quadrangle is the north range, with large, weathered sandstone blocks on the inside face dating from the early 17th century. It was probably a single-storey hall-house, with a screens passage and entrance on the site of the present passage into the courtyard. The fine carved doorway, *c.*1601, decorated with the Pennyman coat of arms, at the entrance to the courtyard, belonged to this house, though it was moved from the south to north side in the late 17th century. The upper storey and the ranges to the east and west were added during the course of the 17th century.

The Old Wing was converted into a service courtyard in the mid-18th century, with staff accommodation on the first floor and service rooms on the ground floor. It functioned in this way until the outbreak of the Second World War, when most of the staff were called away to war work, and a smaller family kitchen was created in the north-west corner of the courtyard. During the early years of the war, the Old Wing was home to a number of local and Spanish refugees and was later occupied by the Royal Army Medical Corps. Afterwards, it served as the headquarters for Joan Littlewood's Theatre Workshop in the late 1940s, as a boarding house for Hungarian refugees in 1957, and a rehearsal space for Ruth Pennyman's 'New Theatre Group' until 1983. In recent years, the Kitchen, Scullery, Larders and Laundry have been partially reconstructed, using inventories and furniture in the house.

The outer courtyard or Laundry Yard (where the toilets are today) was built in the late 18th or early 19th century, with a dairy, bakehouse and other 'out offices'.

The Kitchen in use in the late 19th century

The Kitchen

The Kitchen

The Kitchen and Scullery, in the south range, were constructed in the mid- to late 18th century, creating a quadrangle out of the old U-plan house. There was originally an open roasting fire and spit at the far end of the Kitchen, equipped with a 'meat screen lined with tin' (to reflect heat), 'beef forks', 'steak tongs', 'basting ladles' and 'pricking forks' in

1853. The alcove on the right-hand side probably contained a hot-plate, with its own fire, for boiling and steaming food. In the late 19th century, the roasting fire was replaced with a closed cooking range with ovens (similar to the one in place today) and the hot-plate with a sink, for preparing vegetables.

The Scullery

In the 18th and 19th centuries, this room was used for baking, salting or preserving, and preparing meat and vegetables. Markings in the floor show that there was originally a bread or pastry oven to the right of the door to the Kitchen, and the 1853 inventory refers to a 'salt pot' and a 'sinkstone', for scrubbing and peeling vegetables. From the late 19th century, these activities were moved into the Kitchen, and the Scullery was used principally for washing up and storing crockery.

The Larders

The two small rooms at the east end of the Scullery were used as meat larders in the 1920s and '30s, with wire-mesh screens letting in cold air from the outside, but keeping out flies. The smaller one, known as the 'Butcher's Shop', was for storing uncooked meat, and the larger one for hanging game, though it is currently fitted out as a Dry Larder.

The Laundry

The Laundry was used for mangling, ironing and airing clothes and household linen, once they had been washed in the Scrub Room and dried in the Laundry Yard. It is fitted with a long ironing table, a large airing rack and winch, sliding ventilators at the top of the west wall and half-shutters to provide privacy when needed, for example when washing family underwear. There was originally an open fireplace at the north end, with a small stove, for heating irons (the free-standing stove was installed much later). In the mid-19th century, the Laundry contained a box mangle for pressing clothes and linen, similar to that here today.

Lighting

The gas fittings in this room and the Scrub Room are the remnants of the late 19th-century lighting system. The whole house was fitted with gas lighting in 1872 by James Stovin Pennyman, who was chairman of the North Ormesby Gas Company. The house was converted to electricity in 1924.

The Scrub Room

The Scrub or Wash Room accommodated the wet laundry work, with stone sinks around two walls and drainage channels at the edge

The indoor staff in the 1930s

Until the late 1930s the Pennymans maintained a full indoor staff, at a similar level to the Victorian period: a Butler, Footman, Bootboy, Head Housemaid, two Under-housemaids, Cook, Kitchenmaid and Scullerymaid, as well as three part-time laundry workers, who came in twice a week, once to wash and once to iron. Extra women were employed from the village when there were many visitors, to help with cleaning and preparation of meals, and sewing work was given to Mrs Irwin from Middlesbrough. All the full-time servants lived-in at Ormesby on the first floor of the Old Wing, with the women on one side and the men on the other, except for Mr Crack the Butler, who occupied the East Lodge with his family. Mrs Grubb, the Head Washerwoman, lived in a cottage on Church Lane in Ormesby village.

Colonel and Mrs Pennyman were known as generous employers, and Ormesby Hall was considered one of the best places to work for miles around. Once the staff had completed their work, their free time was their own, as long as they returned to the Old Wing by 10pm in the evening. They ate the same food as the family, and there was always a bowl of fruit on the Servants' Hall table. Mrs Pennyman, in particular, had progressive and egalitarian ideas. She exchanged the plain striped uniform of the Under-housemaids for pretty floral dresses, in colours chosen specially to go with the girls' eyes.

The Laundry

leading to a grille by the outside door, to take away the water. A 'boiling copper' with its own fire pit, for heating water and boiling whites, is built into the alcove to the left of the fireplace. There was formerly a dirty laundry chute in the alcove to the right of the fireplace, running from the first floor of the Old Wing. The door in the east wall opened on to the Laundry Yard, where the clothes and linen were dried.

The Servants' Hall (*present tea-room*)

This served as a staff dining room from the mid–18th to the mid–20th century, furnished with long tables, benches and chairs for the upper servants and, in the 1930s, a three-piece suite and rugs. The fireplace at the north end, with a small side oven and hob, was used for toasting bread, heating water kettles and supplementary cooking. The hooks on the ceiling beam were for leather fire buckets, as a basic fire precaution.

The additional small tea-room was used as the 'Boot House' or 'Shoe Room'.

The garden

The 17th-century garden

Though the 17th-century garden was swept away in the mid-18th century to make way for the present house, it is intriguing for its connection with the Rev. William Lawson, the first original British garden writer. Lawson was Vicar of Ormesby from 1583 to 1635 and wrote two practical books on horticulture, *A New Orchard and Garden* and *The Country House-Wife's Garden*, whilst living here. The latter is the first book in any language written specifically for women gardeners. They are based entirely on his own gardening experience and give useful advice on methods of planting, cultivation of roses, management of fruit trees, beekeeping and garden design. Given Lawson's proximity to the Pennymans and the popularity of his books at the time, it is very likely that he influenced their approach to gardening. The grounds of the old house are first described in a survey of *c.*1715, with 2½ acres of gardens, surrounded by a plantation of ash trees, an avenue, orchard, pond and nursery, which may have developed from Lawson's time.

Tour of the garden

The present lawns and gardens surrounding the house were established in the mid- to late 18th century, with a ha-ha, or sunken wall, on three sides, separating them from the wider parkland. In the late 19th century, the section of the ha-ha wall in front of the house was taken back by 50 metres, and the section at the back cut through with a croquet lawn. The trees on the front lawn, to the right of the main drive, were planted in honour of Frances Pennyman's marriage to Colonel Macbean in 1855.

The gateway on the west side of the house, leading to the flower garden and shrubbery, was taken from the Pennymans' second home, Thornton Hall, about four miles away, in the early 19th century. It initially served as an entrance to the park, opposite the main road to Middlesbrough, but was relocated to the garden about 1936. The ball finials on the gate-piers were intended as globe sundials, and the hour markings are still visible.

On the right, as you enter the garden, are beds of mixed hybrid tea roses, surrounding a

An illustration from A New Orchard and Garden *(1676) by the Rev. William Lawson, who was Vicar of Ormesby and may have advised on the design of the 17th-century garden*

The garden

'heliochronometer', or sophisticated sundial, made by Pilkington Gibbs Ltd in the early 20th century. It is designed to give accurate time through a system of discs and dials. Further scented roses, *Clematis* 'Perle d'Azur', honeysuckle and *Wisteria floribunda* 'Macrobotrys' clothe the south and west walls of the house. The terrace, in the corner between the main house and the Old Wing, is decorated with tubs of *Agapanthus* Headbourne hybrids and surrounded by lavender and scented roses. It is on the site of one of two conservatories, constructed in 1858 and 1884, which together covered the whole of the west wall of the Old Wing. The last of these was demolished about 1965.

To the south of the Old Wing is a short woodland walk, with St Cuthbert's church visible through a break in the planting. A small walnut tree marks the end of the walk, and brings the visitor out on to the croquet lawn, at the far end of the garden. Here, the Pennymans played their favourite game of 'Ormesby Golf Croquet', with a miniature nine-hole golf course laid out on the grass.

The large sunken lawn, to the west of the house, was used for tennis from the 1870s, with a pavilion for spectators hidden amongst the tall hedges on the bank. When the grass was wet, the game was played on the wide gravel paths, until the 1930s, when Colonel Pennyman built hard courts near the old kitchen garden, on the opposite side of Church Lane. The walled kitchen garden, with green- and hot-houses and hot-walls (enclosing passages for the circulation of hot air to provide warmth for exotic fruit trees), and an orchard and plantations beyond, was established in the late 18th century. The land was sold for development after the Second World War, though part of the original stone wall remains behind the houses.

The shrubbery, surrounding the tennis lawn, is planted with Portuguese Laurel, azaleas and hydrangeas. To the left of the Norwegian pine is the entrance to the Holly Walk, leading round the western perimeter of the garden to the exit to the car-park, marked by a pair of Lombardy poplars. Looking out across the ha-ha and car-park, you can see the rear of the unusual late 18th-century quarter-circle piggery, at the back of Grange Farm.

St Cuthbert's church

The parish church of Ormesby, dedicated to the great Northumbrian saint St Cuthbert, is situated within the grounds of Ormesby Hall, with an entrance for villagers on Church Lane. According to legend, St Cuthbert's coffin rested in Ormesby in the late 9th century, on its journey from Lindisfarne to Durham, transported by monks escaping the threat of Viking invasion. The foundations of the present building date from the medieval period, but the nave, vestry and chancel were rebuilt in 1874–5 at the instigation of James Stovin Pennyman by the architect William Serle Hicks, whose firm had offices in Newcastle and Middlesbrough. The project was funded by public subscription; Stovin personally contributed £400. The tower and spire were added by H. L. Hicks in 1907. The family plot is on the left as you enter the churchyard.

The stables

They were completed for Sir James Pennyman, 6th Bt, in 1772, the date inscribed on the bell in the clock-tower. They consist of two quadrangles, connected by a series of three archways, which lead out to the East Lodge and back entrance on Church Lane. The principal quadrangle is the first building you see as you enter the main drive and forms a dramatic prelude before the main house comes into view. It is designed in the late Palladian style, with the main, west façade divided into three sections of three bays each. The central section projects slightly under a pediment and is crowned with a clock-tower and open rotunda containing a bell. The design has been firmly attributed to John Carr of York and is comparable to his stables at Castle Howard, Escrick Park, Ravenfield Hall and Ribston Park, elsewhere in Yorkshire. The round-headed windows in the west façade, linked by a string course, are a particular feature of Carr's work. The clock, which retains its original 18th-century movement, has recently been restored to working order.

The 6th Baronet bred his own race-horses, and the stables originally provided accommodation for over 20 horses, as well as a coach-house and staff accommodation on the second storey. The numbers of horses declined in the 19th century and dwindled to nothing in the early 20th century, when the Pennymans started to use cars: Colonel Pennyman kept a black Talbot with red wire wheels, and his

The stable block was built for Sir James Pennyman, 6th Bt, in 1772

wife a fawn Morris coupé. In the inter-war years, the stable block was let out as a riding school to Mr Boyes of Skelton, who occasionally lent the Colonel a horse for recreational rides. In the mid-1930s, Ruth Pennyman started to put on summer productions of Shakespeare in the stable courtyard, which provided the perfect setting for *Romeo and Juliet* in 1934, with Juliet's balcony in the eastern archway. Today, the Cleveland Mounted Police has its headquarters in the building, so horses remain a feature of the estate.

The park and lodges

The parkland, consisting of 73 hectares (excluding home farm land), stretches away from the gardens at the front and back of the house, and was almost certainly enclosed by the 6th Baronet in the 1770s. It is laid out in a simplified version of the naturalistic style made popular by 'Capability' Brown in the 1760s, with a perimeter band of trees, known as the Pleasure Grounds, cut through with a meandering path, and a copse, known as Round Clump, on the main drive. At the same time, the West Lodge was constructed at the main entrance to the park, probably to a design by John Carr of York, with two classical pavilions and gate-piers, originally crowned with the Pennyman lions (now displayed in the Entrance Hall). The small Tudor Gothic East Lodge, on Church Lane at the back of the stables, was built for the 7th Baronet in 1824 and was traditionally occupied by the family butler or chauffeur.

Soon after the park was created, the 6th Baronet went bankrupt, and the land was let out in small enclosures to local farmers, for growing oats and wheat. It was reclaimed by the 7th Baronet and put back to pasture in 1809. From the Victorian period, the northern part was used by the family and local community for sports, with cricket and football in the summer (the cricket pitch remains) and golf in the winter months. The Pennymans travelled especially to St Andrews in Scotland for golf lessons and commissioned the professional player Hugh Kirkaldy to lay out a

nine-hole course in the park. Bob Hardy, the Head Woodman, was trained up as a caddy and an upper room in the stables was fitted out as a repair shop for clubs. In the 1930s, the park was the venue for the annual Ormesby Horticultural Show, of which Colonel Pennyman was president, and a large political rally and garden fête in 1937, which was attended by the Prime Minister, Neville Chamberlain.

The southern pasture served as grazing land for the cattle from Grange Farm, which is situated on the western boundary of the park. In the 1960s, a new trunk road to Redcar, the A174, was constructed through the southern pasture, a few metres from the end of the garden, though it was carefully hidden in a landscaped cutting with advice from the landscape designer Sylvia Crowe. Since 1961, when the property was given to the National Trust, a large part of the park has once again been let out as farmland.

The heraldic lions now displayed in the Entrance Hall came originally from the park lodges

The estate

Today Ormesby Hall and its parkland are surrounded by urban development, caught up in the suburbs of Middlesbrough. However, it was originally at the centre of a rural farming estate, consisting of 1,207 acres (488 hectares), stretching four miles southwards from the River Tees, from Middle Beck on the east to Marton Beck on the west. The Pennymans owned other farmland elsewhere in the vicinity, including Stainton, Maltby and Sadberge, and together their estates provided them with the bulk of their income until the mid-20th century.

The Ormesby estate was divided into a number of smallholdings and four or five substantial farms, one of which was managed directly by the Pennymans. The Home, or Grange, Farm supplied the family with most of their produce, including meat, cereals, milk and eggs, but, well into the 18th century, the tenant farmers' rents included providing a number of turkeys, geese, hens and eggs as well as coal, mostly at Christmas. In the 17th century, the Hall was also the Home Farm, but in the mid-18th century Grange Farm was built on the west side of the park. The 6th Baronet made considerable improvements to the farm in the 1770s, building an advanced quarter-circle piggery, in which each pig had a separate yard and shelter. He also owned a fine herd of short-horn cattle, including the sire of the great bull 'Hubback', of which it was said in 1821 that 'no bull ever possessed a greater propensity to fatten'.

The Pennymans also owned property in Ormesby village, including a brewery, saddler's shop, carpenter's shop and several cottages, many of which were occupied by estate workers. Most of the old village has been swept away by modern development, but one terrace of 18th-century cottages survives on the corner of Ladgate and Church lanes. It was founded in 1719 by Sir James Pennyman, 3rd Bt, with four almshouses for the poor, and completed in the 1770s with nine more cottages and a 'Publick School House' at the eastern end, which was used by local people until 1904. A further 68 houses were built by Colonel Pennyman on Jubilee Bank in 1936 to commemorate the Silver Jubilee of King

ORMESBY LANE

Ormesby village about 1900

The outdoor staff in the 1930s

The whole of the estate was managed for Colonel Pennyman by a land agent, Captain Pritchett, of the York family of architects, who lived in a house on Ladgate Lane. Under him was a team of estate workers, including the gamekeeper, assistant keeper, estate joiner, apprentice joiner and three woodmen. In addition to their estate work, the woodmen carried out heavy work around the house, including cleaning the carpets by dragging them up and down the front lawn and keeping the fires supplied with logs. Two bricklayers and a labourer were occasionally employed to help with repairs and improvements around the grounds and on the farms. The gardens were maintained by five men, including Mr Imeson the Head Gardener, an Assistant Head Gardener and three boy apprentices. Mr Imeson lived in a cottage on the far side of Church Lane, adjacent to the old kitchen garden.

George V, and at Coronation Green the following year. The Colonel regarded it as a social obligation to provide local people with decent, affordable accommodation and had a letter published in the *Architects Journal* in 1928 on the importance of good design in public housing.

The estate constituted a small, self-contained community, with seventeen households in the late 17th century and 31 by 1862, who regularly gathered together on festive occasions. Sir William Pennyman and his neighbour, William Brown, who owned the other half of the township of Ormesby, provided a feast for all the villagers, with 'beef, pease, salt, mustard, ale and punch', to mark the Coronation of William IV in 1831. From the mid-

19th century, the Pennymans were particularly dedicated landlords, living on their estate all year round and developing a strong relationship with their tenant farmers. They instituted an annual tradition of Rent Dinners for the tenants at Christmas, with roast beef and Yorkshire pudding in the Red Lion pub (later rebuilt as the Fountain). In addition, James Stovin Pennyman organised 'tea drinking' and games for the village schoolchildren on New Year's Day, when they were invited to the house to admire the Christmas decorations. Colonel Pennyman continued the tradition of Rent Dinners into the mid-20th century.

The Ormesby estate started to decrease in size from the mid-19th century. James White Pennyman was still saddled with debts from the 6th Baronet's time and started to lease land at the northern end to industrialists and developers building the new town of Middlesbrough (see p. 41). The family's finances suffered further from agricultural depression in the late 19th century and heavy death duties after the First World War.

In 1925 Colonel Pennyman was forced to sell the remainder of White House Farm to developers and to tenant Grange Farm. Finally, after the Second World War, Berwick Field and Keld House farms, immediately north of Ladgate Lane, were sold to the Council for housing. Grange Farm is now owned by the National Trust and is tenanted, as in the Colonel's time.

(Right) Estate staff and their families in the late 19th century

The Pennymans of Ormesby

The coat of arms on the Old Wing came from the Pennymans' original house on the site, built about 1601

Early history

There have been Pennymans in north Yorkshire since at least the 15th century, when Thomas Pennyman is recorded as a 'gentleman' living in Stokesley, about seven miles from Ormesby Hall. Thomas's great grandson, Robert, was 'hanged, headed and quartered' on the Knavesmire at York for his part in the Northern Rebellion of 1569, fighting against the establishment of the Protestant religion by Elizabeth I. His head was displayed on one of the main gates of the city as a warning to other rebels. The family's fortunes had recovered by 1599, when Robert's nephew, James (d. 1624), was granted a crest to his existing coat of arms, as 'a man famous for his valour … as well as deserving of the State'. He was evidently a

man of some means, purchasing most of the township of Ormesby in 1600–1.

James started to build on his land around 1601. He created a simple stone house, with a hall, screens passage and parlour, which is now incorporated into the Old Wing. It had a fine Jacobean doorcase decorated with the Pennyman coat of arms, which survives today, but was really little more than a large farmhouse. James's son, another James, extended the house with a single-storey service wing on the east side, but all further improvements were postponed in the mid-17th century, as the family became embroiled in the Civil War.

The Pennymans were fiercely loyal to Charles I during the Civil War. At the age of 64, the younger James marshalled troops for the royal army at Stokesley and Guisborough, and opposed the landing of Oliver Cromwell's men at Marske, near Redcar. All three of his sons were active in the royalist cause; the eldest, Sir James (1608–79), was knighted on the battlefield at Durham in 1642 and later commanded a regiment in the King's army. He was forced into exile in Holland in 1644, taking only a servant and two horses, but returned to England in 1645, after King Charles had been finally defeated.

The Restoration of Charles II in 1660 saw the Pennymans being rewarded for their loyalty. Sir James was granted a baronetcy in 1664, and his son, Sir Thomas, 2nd Bt, was appointed High Sheriff of Yorkshire in 1702–3. In 1692 his son, Sir James, 3rd Bt (c.1661–1745), married Mary Warton of Beverley, a substantial heiress from one of the leading families in the East Riding. She introduced the Pennymans to the society of Beverley, which had become the administra-tive centre for the East Riding and where a busy social scene was rapidly developing.

In the late 17th century, Sir Thomas enlarged the old house, building a second storey on to the east wing and a further wing on the west side. He also greatly increased the family estates, buying lands in the locality at Stainton, Hutton, Maltby, Barwicke and Sadberge. The Stainton estate had an existing Jacobean house, called Thornton Hall, which was more substantial than the dwelling at Ormesby. It was initially occupied by the future 3rd Baronet and his wife, and when Sir Thomas died in 1708, it became the principal family residence. The old Ormesby Hall was let out to a yeoman farmer until 1737, when it was reclaimed as a home for the 3rd Baronet's eldest son, James, and his wife, Dorothy.

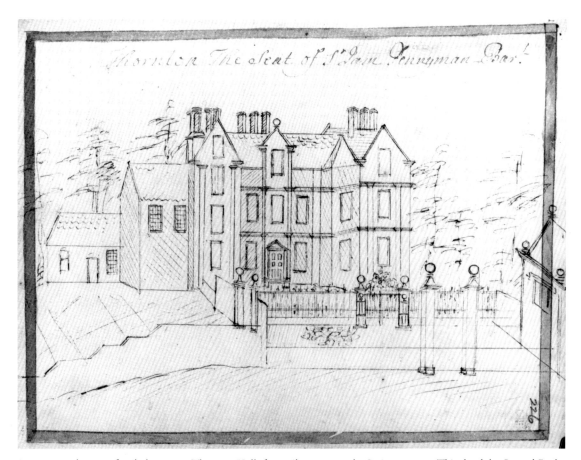

From 1708, the main family home was Thornton Hall, four miles away on the Stainton estate. This sketch by Samuel Buck shows gateposts now in the garden at Ormesby (illustrated on p.27)

The finely carved doorcases in the Gallery were commissioned in the 1740s by Dorothy Pennyman

The house

James Pennyman (1693–1743) married Dorothy Wake, one of the six daughters of William Wake, Archbishop of Canterbury, in 1722. The young couple moved into Normanby Hall, a few miles east of Ormesby, which they leased from their cousin, William Pennyman, as the old house was considered too old-fashioned and inconvenient to provide a family home. However, in 1737 the situation changed, as Dorothy's father died, probably leaving her one-sixth of his fortune (about £15,000). Fortified with this inheritance, James and Dorothy reclaimed the old hall, converting it into a service wing and starting to build the present house on an adjacent site in the modern Palladian style.

John Graves, who visited Ormesby in 1808, described the hall 'as a neat modern mansion, built by Mrs Pennyman'. The Pennymans themselves had little history of house-building, and it is quite likely that Dorothy provided the enthusiasm as well as the finance for the project. Dorothy's father had been an important patron of architecture. He also headed the second New Churches Commission, which brought him into contact with new architectural ideas and modern architects, including Colen Campbell, a protégé of Lord Burlington, who dedicated a church design to Archbishop Wake. However it started, the project was certainly completed by Dorothy, as James died in 1743, two years before his father, leaving her to supervise the final stages of construction and the fitting-up of the interior.

Unfortunately, there is very little documentation on the building of Ormesby Hall, and it has not yet been possible to identify with certainty the architect involved. However, it may have been the work of Colonel James Moyser, a little-known gentleman-architect from Beverley, who was distantly related to the Pennymans by marriage. Moyser was a friend of Lord Burlington, the great champion of the Palladian style in England, and worked for the Winns at Nostell Priory, near Wakefield, about 1735. He favoured a simple version of the Palladian style similar to that at Ormesby Hall. The Ormesby façade also bears a striking resemblance to that at Kirby Hall in Yorkshire, where Moyser advised in the 1740s.

Once the building work was finished, Dorothy lived on her own at Ormesby Hall until she died in 1754. Her Will, dated 1753, shows that she had an unusually strong attachment to her house, as it carefully details 'the brass locks fixed on the doors ... marble chimney pieces, hearth slabs, chimney pieces, dutch tiles and bells', which she had chosen ten years before. She and James had no children, and the 3rd Baronet was succeeded in turn by his second son, William, 4th Bt, in 1745, and his third son, Warton, 5th Bt, in 1768. Neither William nor Warton lived at Ormesby, but divided their time between Thornton Hall and houses in Beverley. Ormesby Hall was thus left empty until 1770, when Warton was succeeded by his nephew, James, who once again established it as the principal family home.

The garden front

The rise and fall of the 6th Baronet

Sir James Pennyman, 6th Bt (1736–1808), grew up in Beverley and was educated at Westminster School, London, and Christ Church, Oxford. In 1756 he married Elizabeth, daughter of Sir Henry Grey of Howick in Northumberland. By the time he inherited the family estates in 1770, he was already well established in Beverley society, with a substantial villa, Lairgate Hall (now owned by a private business) and an emerging political career in the town.

Sir James was described by Lord Rockingham, the most powerful Whig aristocrat in Yorkshire, as 'a very good sort of man ...with a thumping landed property, who is exceedingly anxious to get into Parliament'. With Rockingham's support, Sir James was elected MP for Scarborough in 1770 and successfully contested Beverley in 1774, which he represented for over twenty years. However, he seldom spoke in the House of Commons and transferred his support to the Tories after Rockingham's death. In any case, elections in Beverley were rarely decided on matters of party politics, as they were notorious for their corruption in the late 18th century. Candidates were expected to bribe the voters with free drinks and cash payments, spending up to £3,000 of their own money on expenses. The successful candidate was also required to contribute generously to the poor and to public works, and to entertain the Freemen of the city on

special occasions. Sir James clearly struggled with his payments, as the Clerk of the Council was asked to write to him in 1779, for 'the annual sum of £10 paid to the Master of the Grammar School, which subscription was five years in arrears'.

By the late 18th century, Beverley had much to offer a wealthy young man, with a theatre, assembly rooms, cockpits and a busy horse-racing calendar. Sir James enjoyed all its delights, but was particularly keen on horse-racing, serving as a steward at Beverley, York and Northallerton race-courses. He bred his own race-horses, including North Star, which won him 1,200 guineas in 1772, and his pea-green racing colours became known throughout the north of England. In 1767 he

'Wicked Sir James' Pennyman, 6th Bt, whose extravagance forced him to sell the contents of Ormesby in 1792; attributed to Sir Joshua Reynolds, 1762 (Dining Room)

was elected to the committee for building a new grandstand on Beverley race-course, which was demolished in 1925, but may well have been designed by John Carr of York. Sir James won and lost considerable sums at the races and was said to have been addicted to gambling. According to family tradition, he would even gamble on rain drops running down the window pane, when there was nothing better to bet on, and he was nick-named 'the Wicked Sir James' for frittering away the family fortune.

As soon as he inherited in 1770, the 6th Baronet started to spend money on his properties. He bought back the eastern part of the township of Ormesby in 1771, which had passed out of the family in the early 17th century, for the massive sum of £47,500. At the same time, he refurbished the interiors of his houses at Ormesby and Lairgate with fine Neo-classical plasterwork ceilings, and rebuilt the stables at Ormesby on a much grander scale, to accommodate his string of race-horses. He also laid out the parkland at Ormesby, commissioning new gates and lodges at the main entrance to the park, and making substantial improvements to Grange Farm.

The architectural work was almost certainly carried out by John Carr of York, who would have been well known to the 6th Baronet through his commissions in Beverley. The plasterwork ceiling in the Dining Room at Lairgate Hall, in particular, is almost identical to one designed by Carr at Thirsk Hall, which was executed by the craftsman John Henderson. At this time, Carr was the principal architect for the gentry in the north of England, designing many accomplished Neo-classical interiors in the spirit of Robert Adam.

By 1779, Sir James had debts of over £50,000, the equivalent of many millions in modern money. In 1781 he was forced to auction Lairgate Hall and its contents, and in 1789 to sell the eastern part of the Ormesby estate for less than the original purchase price. The western part of the estate was legally entailed and so could not be sold, but the contents of Ormesby Hall were auctioned in

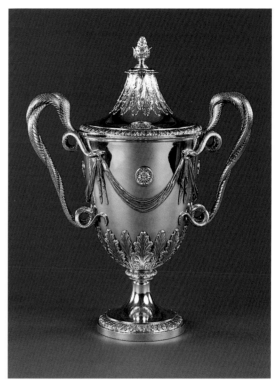

The silver race cup in the Dining Room was commissioned in 1772 by Sir James Pennyman, who built the stables and gambled away a fortune at the races

1792, and the gardens and greenhouses were let to a local man, Henry Brown, for £30 per annum. Even the lead water-pipes were removed for sale. It is said that Thornton Hall was demolished c.1805 to salvage the building materials and that the interior fittings of Ormesby were saved only by the efforts of an elderly serving woman. According to the travel writer William Hutton, who visited the area in 1809, she 'never stirred out or admitted any soul within the premises, but sustained a siege of many years ... and was continually supplied with food and other necessaries, by a basket and string let down from a window'. Meanwhile, Sir James Pennyman had moved to lodgings in Richmond, Surrey, where he married his second wife, Mary, and died in 1808. In a final act of extravagance, his body was returned for burial at the family vault at Thornton, at the enormous cost of £501 15s.

The 7th Baronet

Sir James's eldest son, William, the 7th and last Baronet, inherited Ormesby in a much diminished and impoverished state. He paid off the bailiffs, renewed the lead piping at a cost of £400 in 1809, and built the small Tudor Gothic East Lodge in 1824, but made few other substantial improvements to the estate. He lived a relatively modest life on a small sinecure from his mother's family, spending the winter months in lodgings in Beverley, and returning to Ormesby in May in a hired coach and four, with a Grange Farm waggon to carry his belongings. According to family tradition, his only personal extravagance was snuff, which was procured for him by the old gamekeeper, Cameron, on his weekly visit to Stokesley to buy family supplies. He died without children in 1852 and was succeeded by his aunt's eldest grandson, James White Worsley, a cousin of the Worsleys of Hovingham Hall, near Helmsley. James White Worsley was initially uncertain whether to accept his inheritance, as the Ormesby estate was still heavily mortgaged from the time of the 6th Baronet, and all Sir William's personal property, including the furniture and furnishings at Ormesby, had been left to his sister's family. However, he was swayed by the belief that the fresh air of Teesside would be beneficial to the delicate health of his only son, James, and moved into the house in 1853, buying back several items of furniture from his uncle's estate. He changed his surname to Pennyman by royal licence, but the baronetcy became extinct, as it could not be passed down through the female line.

The development of Middlesbrough

When the Worsley Pennymans moved into Ormesby Hall in the mid-19th century, the landscape of Teesside was rapidly changing. The effects of the Industrial Revolution were particularly marked in this rural region, where the tiny hamlet of Middlesbrough was trans-

James Stovin Pennyman, who created the present Dining Room and Drawing Room in the 1870s; coloured chalk drawing by G.L. Browning, 1851 (North Bedroom)

formed into a centre of industry in a matter of decades. From the 1830s, Middlesbrough was developed as a commercial port for the export of coal and timber, and in the 1850s, with the discovery of iron ore in the Cleveland Hills, it rapidly expanded as a centre for the iron and later steel trade. It had one of the fastest growing urban populations in Victorian England, rising from 7,431 in 1851 to 75,532 in 1891. The view from Ormesby Hall, described by John Graves in 1808 as a 'pleasing prospect of the mouth and winding course of the river Tees', was transformed by blast furnaces and heavy machinery on the northern boundary of the estate.

James White Pennyman was better equipped for the modern age than many of his contemporaries amongst the gentry. He came from a rather impoverished branch of the Worsley family and was forced to earn his own living, first as an officer in the Corps of Engineers, then as Intendant of Public Works on the Ionian islands of Greece, and finally as Surveyor of Bridges for the North Riding, from 1837. His son, James Stovin Pennyman, grew up next to a railway line in the Yorkshire village of Thornton-le-Moor, where he spent many hours train-spotting, noting down their numbers in his early diaries. Stovin later attended the newly founded University of Durham, graduating in Civil and Mining Engineering in 1853, the first course of its kind in the country. His diaries from the 1850s show that the Pennymans viewed the development of Middlesbrough with a great deal of interest and excitement. The family and their guests regularly visited the ironstone mines, iron works, docks and shipyards, and walked the length of the new Middlesbrough to Guisborough railway line in the company of the resident engineer.

Unlike their neighbours, the Ward-Jacksons of Normanby Hall, who founded the docks at Hartlepool, the Pennymans were never directly involved in the development of the new industries. Nevertheless, the expansion of Middlesbrough brought them some financial stability, as their land increased in value as a prime building site. In the mid-1850s, James White Pennyman leased land to the new railway company and to Cochrane's iron-works at the northern end of the estate. He also started to develop the new town of North Ormesby, on part of White House Farm, to accommodate the influx of iron-workers to the area. James Stovin Pennyman, who succeeded his father in 1870, owned shares in a number of the new local businesses, including the North Ormesby Gas Company. He also was a director of the North Eastern Banking Company, founded in 1872.

With the money from the leasing of land, the Pennymans were able to repair and improve the remainder of the farming estate, which was still in a dilapidated condition. James White paid off the mortgages and put in place a rolling programme for the laying of field drains on the tenant farms. He also started to improve and modernise Ormesby Hall (see p. 3), installing gas lighting in 1872 and a steam-driven pump to improve the water supply in 1879. The house was finally converted to electricity by Stovin's grandson, Colonel Pennyman, in 1924.

The Drawing Room in the late 19th century. The gas lights were installed in 1872

Life at Ormesby, 1850–1924

Through all the upheaval of industrialisation, the peaceful tenor of country-house life continued remarkably unchanged. Many of the newly rich industrialists and businessmen of Middlesbrough, including the Peases, Bolckows, Vaughans and Bells, built their own country houses in the area and were apparently absorbed into landed society. Stovin's diaries record that the Pennymans mingled happily with the new families at tennis parties, dances and private theatricals. From the 1860s, Ormesby was known for its theatrical productions, performed in the dull January months for an audience of local friends and neighbours, with the dress rehearsals open to the Ormesby villagers. Their first performance was of *A Regular Fix* by Maddison Morton, with 'a charade by a well-known troupe of grandchildren', for which James White Pennyman 'put up a nice little theatre in the Hall' in 1864.

Unlike their ancestors, the Victorian Pennymans lived at Ormesby all year round and immersed themselves in local life. James Stovin Pennyman was a captain in the 1st North Yorkshire Volunteer Artillery and a leading member of the Church Choral Union

Ormesby has a long tradition of theatre. In 1873 the family performed one of W. S. Gilbert's less famous solo efforts, Creatures of Impulse

(Far left) James Worsley Pennyman succeeded to Ormesby in 1896; painted by C.S.V. Harcourt in 1904 (Entrance Hall)

(Left) Dora Maria, née Beaumont, who married James Worsley Pennyman in 1882; painted by C.S.V. Harcourt in 1904 (Entrance Hall)

for Cleveland, which staged a choral festival at Redcar with over 300 performers. He encouraged adult education in the region, lecturing personally on 'Geology', 'Columbus & the discovery of America' and 'Currents of Oceans and Atmosphere' at Ormesby Village School. He also co-founded the 'Cleveland Book Hawking Society', which sponsored a licensed 'bookhawker' to drive a small lending library around north Yorkshire in a specially constructed cart.

Stovin's eldest son, James Worsley Pennyman (1856–1924), trained as a barrister in London, but according to *his* son, Colonel Pennyman, he lacked drive and 'never in all his life got a Brief'. He returned to Ormesby when Stovin died in 1896, serving as an Alderman and Chairman of the Finance Committee for the North Riding County Council. He was succeeded in 1924 by his eldest son, James (later Colonel) Pennyman.

North Ormesby

Between 1853 and 1924, the Pennymans developed the town of North Ormesby, just to the south of the River Tees. They leased, and eventually sold, plots of land within the overall street pattern to a variety of builders and developers, who initially constructed modest two-up, two-down houses, for rent by local ironworkers, and later, more substantial three-storey properties to accommodate professional people escaping from the centre of Middlesbrough. The overall arrangement of the working-class housing was slightly better than in Middlesbrough, with wide back alleys between the terraces, providing good access for refuse carts.

The Pennymans took great interest in the development of the new community, which they initially considered as part of their own. They founded the Smeaton Street School, contributed to the building of Holy Trinity church, and donated £900 towards a new cemetery in 1870. They also provided a site for the new Cottage Hospital in 1861, and in 1875 started the North Ormesby Market, whose tolls were given to the hospital fund.

As North Ormesby expanded in size in the 1860s and '70s, dwarfing the old community of Ormesby village, it outgrew the support of the Pennyman family. The new inhabitants were more critical than the traditional villagers, openly criticising Stovin Pennyman over his policy for the Smeaton Street School at a Local Board meeting in 1872. In the late 19th

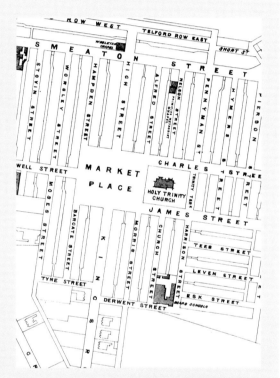

North Ormesby was developed by the Pennymans between 1853 and 1924

century, the Pennymans handed control of the school and other institutions to the local authority, and in 1913 the town was included within the borough of Middlesbrough. Many of the original houses have now been demolished, but the street names, including 'Pennyman', 'Worsley' and 'Stovin', commemorate the founding family.

The 20th century

Colonel James Pennyman

James (always known as Jim) Pennyman
(1883–1961) was educated at Eton and
Cambridge, with the intention that he should
go into the law. However, he was a practical
rather than an intellectual man and accepted a
commission in the King's Own Scottish
Border Regiment in 1905. On the outbreak of
the First World War, his regiment was one
of the first in action, but he was severely
wounded in 1914 and eventually retired from
the army, as a major, in 1920, on the grounds
of poor health. His military training and war
service remained a strong influence throughout
his life. Looking for another down-to-earth
activity, Jim enrolled in agricultural college at
Cambridge and settled with his wife, Mary
(née Powell), at a farm on family land at
Stainton. Tragedy struck in 1924, when Mary
died in childbirth, a few months before James
Worsley Pennyman, and Jim spent two
unhappy years at Ormesby Hall, grieving with
his mother and sister. Everything changed in
1926, when Ruth Knight, the daughter of a
Devon vicar, came to stay. Jim was a conven-
tional country landowner and Ruth a rebellious
art school graduate, but they fell in love and
married within a matter of months. Their

*Colonel James
Pennyman;
painted in 1958
(Drawing
Room)*

partnership, with its peculiar blend of tradition
and creativity, characterised life at Ormesby for
the following 35 years.

Jim Pennyman was deeply committed to
his role as a country landowner. He was a
hands-on farmer at Stainton and Grange Farm
at Ormesby until the mid-1920s. Afterwards,
he maintained a close relationship with all his
tenant farmers, and enjoyed all the practical
aspects of estate management, especially
forestry work. He also strongly believed in the
traditional duties of the landowner, as a leader
within the local community. He acted as
Chairman of the Cleveland Conservative
Association, Deputy Lieutenant of Yorkshire
and commanded a battalion of the National
Defence Corps, as a Lieutenant Colonel,
during the Second World War. He also served
as a magistrate on the north-eastern circuit
for 52 years, finally retiring in 1959 at the age
of 75. He was awarded an OBE for his public
works.

Jim was deeply worried by the Great
Depression in the late 1920s, which left
thousands of Teesside miners out of work.
Wishing to be of practical help and soothe
tensions in the region, he initiated two
schemes to alleviate their hardship.

The Cleveland Unemployed Miners' Association

Jim's first venture was a co-operative market
garden and livestock scheme, which started at
the end of 1931. He rented three plots of
scrubland near the mining villages of Margrove
Park, Charlton, Boosbeck and Lingdale, each
of which was to be run collectively by a group
of miners, producing fruit and vegetables and
raising livestock. Sixty unemployed men
pledged their labour in reclaiming the harsh
moorland and were paid with a proportion of
the produce. Jim gathered a wide range of
support for his venture and raised money
for basic stock and equipment through
subscriptions from local gentry and business
families. His brother-in-law, John Connolly,
managed the project, and Ruth organised

In February 1933 Jim Pennyman (on the left) showed Prince George the depressed areas of East Cleveland, where the unemployment rate was then 91%

sewing and knitting groups for the miners' wives in Rushby's Rooms, a disused shop in Boosbeck.

Boosbeck Industries

The second venture started as a small carpentry workshop in Rushby's Rooms, where the miners' sons made beehives and cold frames for their smallholdings, and simple furniture for their homes. It developed into a small business, Boosbeck Industries, managed by Bernard Aylward, a young Quaker craft teacher from Bootham school in York, who was taken on by Jim in 1933. Aylward, who went on to become President of the National Association of Design Education, designed 'simple, straightforward and robust' furniture, in oak, walnut or painted wood, which was

constructed by his apprentices for sale. The young men and boys initially received a proportion of the takings and later a regular wage for their work, as sales picked up. Boosbeck Industries enjoyed some commercial success, but it was never really financially viable, as Jim paid Aylward's wages of £200 a year from his own pocket. It folded in 1937, when the mines started to reopen.

A laundry basket made by Boosbeck Industries, a pioneering employment scheme set up by the Pennymans during the Great Depression of the 1930s

The Cleveland Workcamps

The Cleveland project developed in a unique and surprising way through the Pennymans' friendship with Rolf Gardiner, an idealistic young man who visited Cleveland in the mid-1920s to study the ancient 'Sword Dance' tradition. He was befriended by Ruth Pennyman and frequently stayed at Ormesby Hall. Gardiner believed that the problems of industrial society could be solved only by a return to the land and traditional cultural roots. He had been involved with the Rover Scouts at university and was greatly impressed by the German Youth Movement, with its emphasis on outdoor activity. He also felt strongly that the northern nations, including Germany and Britain, had a natural cultural affinity and should heal their rift after the First World War. Many of Gardiner's ideas were too radical and romantic for Colonel Pennyman, but he encouraged Jim in setting up his land-resettlement scheme and persuaded him to incorporate an element of cultural regeneration.

In the summer of 1931, Gardiner organised a musical tour of Yorkshire, bringing together a German youth choir from Frankfurt, conducted by Georg Goetsch, Morris dancers from Dorset, and sword dancers from east Cleveland. Sixty performers used Ormesby Hall as a base for their rehearsals, with the Drawing Room as a music room, the Dining Room as a refectory, and the lofts over the stables as dormitories. In the following year, Gardiner and Goestch returned to Cleveland to participate in Jim's land scheme, with a work-camp of German, Scandinavian and English students. The aim of the project was to bring the students and miners together, in clearing the scrub land for cultivation during the day, and in cultural activities in the evening, including folk dancing and community singing.

(Right) Unemployed miners and German students digging the land together during the 1933 workcamp

(Below) Morris dancers at Ormesby during Rolf Gardiner's musical tour in the summer of 1931

Michael Tippett on Teesside

The workcamp attracted a number of radical young people, including Michael Tippett, then a struggling young composer in London. Tippett, who espoused Marxist politics and was keen to engage with the working classes, joined the second workcamp in September 1932. In this way, Ormesby gained an unexpected association with one of the most important British composers of the 20th century.

Tippett's experience on Teesside proved crucial to his development as a man and an artist. Here, he met the artist Wilf Franks, who introduced him to Trotskyism and to whom he later dedicated his First String Quartet. He also composed his first original opera, *Robin Hood*, for the fifth workcamp in 1934, with a libretto by Ruth Pennyman and David Ayerst, under the pseudonym 'David Michael Pennyless'. The opera was largely performed by local people, with the male chorus provided by the Boosbeck and District Miners' Male Voice Choir and women's voices from local choirs. Some of the music from *Robin Hood* was recycled in the suite he wrote in 1948 to celebrate the birth of Prince Charles.

Michael Tippett composed his first opera for the 1934 Ormesby workcamp

The cast of The Winter's Tale, *performed at Ormesby in 1933*

Ruth Pennyman and the Arts at Ormesby

Ruth Knight attended St John's Wood Art College in London in 1914 and turned to theatre and stage design in the 1920s, collaborating with other well-to-do young artists and actors on plays and Elizabethan masques at Eton College, Hatfield House and her father's rectory at Upton Pyne. She was a typical wayward vicar's daughter, espousing atheism and a brand of left-wing politics which was fashionable amongst intellectuals and artists at the time. In the 1920s and '30s, she claimed to be a Communist, though she never joined the Party and David Ayerst recalls that she was 'rather wild in all various sorts of ideas'. She was also spirited, generous and charming, enjoying the company of all kinds of people and in 1926 she swept into Jim Pennyman's life like a breath of fresh air. Their wedding was itself a theatrical event, with the playing of Elizabethan music and the bride and her attendants in medieval dress.

Though Ruth and Jim were apparently very different characters, they formed a remarkably united partnership at Ormesby. When asked to explain how their relationship worked,

Ruth replied: 'It's fairly easy really. He is Pre-industrial revolution: I am Post.' If they disagreed over politics, they usually found some common ground: during the Spanish Civil War, Ruth was staunchly anti-Franco and travelled to Spain in 1936 to help the Communist cause, even though the Colonel forbade it. However, later that year, he was supporting her in a project to assist Basque refugees escaping from Franco's forces. They

Ruth Pennyman, who made Ormesby a lively centre for the arts; painted in 1958 (Drawing Room)

borrowed Hutton Hall on Teesside, which had been standing empty, and furnished it to accommodate 20 Basque children. With the help of a local Spanish dancer, Ruth trained the children as a singing and dancing troupe, which toured in Switzerland and the north-east of England. When Hutton closed at the beginning of the Second World War, the Pennymans took some of the children into the Old Wing at Ormesby.

Ruth's greatest achievement was in reviving the 19th-century tradition of theatre at Ormesby, on a much larger scale. She started work in the 1930s, producing three Shakespeare plays in the grounds to raise funds for the new village hall. Her first production, of *The Winter's Tale*, was performed on the tennis lawn in 1933, using the silver birch and copper beech trees as props. The cast was entirely composed of local people, with the main parts taken by actors from the Middlesbrough Little Theatre, the crowd scenes played by Ormesby villagers and madrigals sung by the Ormesby Glee Club. Jim Pennyman appeared in a cameo role as a herald riding a horse. Her second production, of *Romeo and Juliet* in 1934, was more ambitious, with a covered stage and raised seating constructed by the estate joiner in the stable courtyard. In this case, the lead roles were played by theatrical friends of Ruth, with Martin Browne (later a producer at Sadler's Wells) as Romeo and Mary Casson (Sybil Thorndike's daughter) as Juliet. Her third production, of *Agincourt* (adapting scenes from *Henry V*), appeared on the croquet lawn in 1935. This play, with its heroic military theme, was Jim's particular favourite; he played the Duke of Exeter.

The final years

In the 1940s and '50s, Ruth expanded her theatrical activities, directing mimes, plays and dances for the Women's Institute and Hovingham Drama Festivals. She wrote her own plays, including *Hot from Heaven* and *Hunter's Moon*, which was awarded 'Best Play

of the Year' in the British Drama League competition. She continued her productions of Shakespeare at Ormesby, with *Much Ado About Nothing*, *The Taming of the Shrew* and *Henry V* in the stable courtyard, and *A Midsummer Night's Dream* in the garden. She also founded two local drama clubs, the New Theatre Group and the Ormesby and Eston Guild of Arts, which put on plays in the village hall and concerts in the Entrance Hall at Ormesby. Ruth welcomed at Ormesby anybody who was interested in the arts, and many local people still remember Ruth's drama groups with great affection, as they opened up a world of music and theatre.

Ruth and Jim did not have any children, and when Colonel Pennyman died in 1961, he bequeathed Ormesby Hall, its park and home farm to the National Trust. Ruth lived on in the house until her death in 1983, continuing her theatrical work at Ormesby throughout the 1960s and '70s, with the support of the National Trust. Family connections are still maintained through Jim's cousin, Bill Hugonin, who lives in Northumberland and served for many years on a number of National Trust committees.

Joan Littlewood at Ormesby

In 1946 the Pennymans offered the Old Wing as a base to Joan Littlewood and Ewan MacColl's experimental 'Theatre Workshop', which they had recently seen perform in Middlesbrough. Joan Littlewood described Ormesby as 'a wonderfully relaxed setting in which the imagination could run riot'. Ruth recalled that 'Jim and [Joan] got on like a house on fire – she amused him immensely and he admired her strength of character'. However, the group also caused him considerable anxiety, with their illicit affairs and dangerous experiments with electric wiring and creative lighting effects. They were eventually given their notice in 1947, leaving behind them, in Ruth's words, 'a trail of scandal, debt and inspiration'.

The Pennymans of Ormesby

JAMES PENNYMAN (d. 1624) =
buys Ormesby 1600–1

Sir JAMES PENNYMAN = (1) Catharine Kingsley
(1579–1655) | m.1603

Sir JAMES PENNYMAN, 1st Bt = Elizabeth Norcliffe (1612–78)
(1608–79) cr. Bt 1664 | m.1632

Sir THOMAS PENNYMAN, 2nd Bt* = Frances Lowther
(1642–1708) | m.1661

Sir JAMES PENNYMAN, 3rd Bt = Mary Warton (d. 1725, aged 73)
(c.1661–1745) | m. 1692

JAMES PENNYMAN = DOROTHY WAKE	Sir WILLIAM	Sir WARTON PENNYMAN-	Ralph
(1693–1743) (d. 1754, aged 55)	PENNYMAN,	WARTON, 5th Bt	Pennyman*
builder of the house m. 1722	4th Bt	(c.1701–70)	(1702–68)
dau. of Archbishop	(1695–1768)	= Charlotte Hotham	= Bridget Gee*
Wake		(d. 1771)	(d. 1774)
		m. 1735	m. 1732

'Wicked Sir JAMES' PENNYMAN, 6th Bt* = (1) Elizabeth Grey m. 1756   Dorothy = Rev. James
(1736–1808) | (2) Mary Maleham (d. 1815) m. 1801 | Worsely

Sir WILLIAM HENRY PENNYMAN, = Charlotte Robinson   Col. James Worsley = Lydia White
7th Bt (d. 1848, aged 82)   (d. 1807) | (d. 1832)
(1764–1852) m. before 1802 | m. 1789

JAMES WHITE WORSLEY PENNYMAN = Frances Stovin
(1792–1870) | (1792–1869)
took Pennyman name on inheriting Ormesby in 1852 | m. 1828

JAMES STOVIN PENNYMAN = Mary Coltman
(1830–96) | m. 1855

JAMES WORSLEY PENNYMAN = Dora Maria Beaumont
(1856–1924) | m. 1882

Col. JAMES PENNYMAN* = (1) Mary Powell (d. 1924)   Dorothy
(1883–1961)   (2) Ruth Knight* (1894–1983) m. 1926   (1889–1948)
bequeathed Ormesby to National Trust 1961

* Asterisk denotes a portrait on show in the house